W9-AUY-479

How-To Guides for Fiendish Rulers

A Pharaoh's Guide

Thanks to the creative team:
Senior Editor: Alice Peebles
Consultant: John Haywood
Fact checker: Kate Mitchell
Design: www.collaborate.agency

Original edition copyright 2016 by Hungry Tomato Ltd.
Copyright © 2017 by Lerner Publishing Group, Inc.
Hungry Tomato™ is a trademark of Lerner Publishing Group, Inc.

All rights reserved. International copyright secured. No part of
this book may be reproduced, stored in a retrieval system, or
transmitted in any form or by any means—electronic, mechanical,
photocopying, recording, or otherwise—without the prior written
permission of Lerner Publishing Group, Inc., except for the
inclusion of brief quotations in an acknowledged review.

Hungry Tomato™
A division of Lerner Publishing Group, Inc.
241 First Avenue North
Minneapolis, MN 55401 USA

For reading levels and more information,
look up this title at www.lernerbooks.com.

Main body text set in Blokletters Balpen 9/13.
Typeface provided by LeFly Fonts.

Library of Congress Cataloging-in-Publication Data

Names: Chambers, Catherine, 1954- author. | Pentney, Ryan, illustrator.
Title: A pharaoh's guide / Catherine Chambers ; Illustrated by: Ryan
Pentney.
Description: Minneapolis : Hungry Tomato, 2017.
Identifiers: LCCN 2016018698 (print) | LCCN 2016021071 (ebook) | ISBN
9781512415490 (lb : alk. paper) | ISBN 9781512430738 (pb : alk. paper) |
ISBN 9781512427059 (eb pdf)
Subjects: LCSH: Pharaohs—Juvenile literature. | Egypt—Politics and
government—To 332 B.C.—Juvenile literature. | Egypt—Civilization—To 332
B.C.—Juvenile literature. | Egypt—Social conditions—Juvenile literature.
Classification: LCC DT61 .C427 2017 (print) | LCC DT61 (ebook) | DDC
932/.01—dc23

LC record available at https://lccn.loc.gov/2016018698

Manufactured in the United States of America
1-39909-21379-8/2/2016

How-To Guides for Fiendish Rulers

A Pharaoh's Guide

by Catherine Chambers
Illustrated by Ryan Pentney

HUNGRY
TOMATO.

CONTENTS

Writing Down My Rules   6

How to Become a Pharaoh   8

Ruling this Life and the Next   10

My Greatest Power   12

Making Cities and Statues   14

Building My Tomb   16

How I Keep Everyone in Place   18

The Importance of FACTS   20

Becoming Very Rich   22

Being a Bad Neighbor   24

My Powerful Death   26

Gods and Goddesses   28

Ten More Fiendish Pharaohs   30

Index   32

Writing Down My Rules

I am a pharaoh and have reigned over Egypt for many years. This means that I am very wise, which is why MY SUBJECTS MUST ALWAYS OBEY ME. My knowledge is tremendous. So I thought the next pharaoh, my son, should learn from me. This is why I am writing down my rules with my my vizier—my special adviser.

MY RULES MUST BE WRITTEN PROPERLY. This is a great rule in itself. My vizier and I do not write them all down by ourselves, of course. A row of scribes sits in front of us, and my loyal vizier makes sure they write everything accurately. I do not want any sly hieroglyphic jokes among my golden nuggets of wisdom.

I am quite old now and still very attractive. It is amazing what a long wig and a false beard can do. MY SUBJECTS MUST ALWAYS SHOW ME ADMIRATION. But I do have a lot of aches and pains. They remind me that I will be passing into the afterlife one day. I call in my priests to tell me when my life on Earth will end. They study the stars and do a lot of equations. Then they make offerings to gods and goddesses. It takes ages. And even after all this, they cannot tell me for sure. So I tell them all to go away—NOW!

This leaves me feeling quite ill. The vizier sends for the royal doctor. MY DOCTOR MUST HELP ME LIVE LONGER. My biggest pain is in my head. So the doctor takes off my wig and lays his hands on a bald patch. He tells me that the four channels leading to the bald patch are blocked. He recommends I take frankincense, yellow ocher, and dung. This will make me vomit and clear the channels. Perfect.

But wait! I can hear drums. It's the Sed festival, celebrating my thirty-year reign as pharaoh. I completely forgot. I must go out and run beside the sacred Apis bull to prove that I can reign for even longer. Ah, I feel so much better.

The scribes have laid down their brushes. The vizier collects the scrolls. My work is done. I know my son will appreciate these rules. I hope you do too. OR ELSE!

How to Become a Pharaoh

I am the mighty pharaoh of all Egypt. That means I am very powerful and extremely rich. I rule over a huge territory that stretches from the Mediterranean Sea in the north to Nubia in the south. *Pharaoh* actually means "royal palace." The bigger the palace, the more powerful I appear to my cowering subjects. It helps them understand that I make the rules.

You may wonder how

I BECAME THE MIGHTY PHARAOH.

I am the son of a pharaoh and his Great Wife, so I followed the rules and inherited my title. We pharaohs have several wives, but the Great Wife is the most important. I chose mine because she comes from a noble and very rich family. Wealth is power.

I just love power.

Now that I am pharaoh,
I CAN CHANGE THE RULES WHENEVER I WANT.
So I am going to pass my title on to the son of
my favorite wife. She's way below my Great Wife
in status, but I get along with her better. It
helps to be a man to become a pharaoh,
but there have been some very
powerful female pharaohs too. But
I have no daughters—yet.

YOU MAY WONDER HOW YOU CAN TELL I AM THE PHARAOH.
Well, it is obvious who I am when I
emerge from my palace and visit my
lands. You cannot miss me as I wear
the most gorgeous clothes. I make
sure that no one else looks like me.
There are dress codes for every class
in society, which I can change whenever
I like. I enjoy seeing peasants and building workers in their simple
white flax clothes. Simple for them is good. As for me, I drip with gold
jewelry studded with precious stones. A gold cobra symbol curls around
my crown. My subjects believe it spits flames at our enemies. Of
course, I don't actually mix with my subjects.

Fiendish Fact File
- Powerful Ancient Egypt was created through warfare when King Narmer, or Menes, united north and south Egypt in about 3100 BCE.

- Ramesses II was one of the most fiendish pharaohs. He ruled for sixty-six years, from 1279 to 1213 BCE. This was so long that his first three sons died before he did. His fourth son, Merneptah, succeeded him.

Ruling this Life and the Next

> I am the god Horus, protector of the Ruler of Egypt!

As pharaoh, I am half man, half god, the son of the sun god Ra. Because I am divine, my subjects must obey me. No one has the right to defy the gods, and I don't let them forget it. Only I can connect them to the gods, and this gives me great control over them. Unfortunately, I cannot seem to control the priests who run the temples of the gods.

Fiendish Fact File

- Pharaohs were first seen as gods during the Second Dynasty of Egypt (2890-2670 BCE). King Raneb, also called Nebra, began this powerful tradition.

- Grand temples were designed only in the New Kingdom (about 1550–1070 BCE).

- Wadjet, the cobra goddess, protected Lower Egypt near the Nile Delta. Nekhbet, a vulture goddess, protected Upper Egypt. They were known as the Two Ladies.

I REALLY WISH THOSE PRIESTS WOULD STICK TO MY RULES.

But I have little say in how they are appointed, and I cannot afford to upset them. That's a very risky business. They help me stay in power when things go wrong—like when we lose a battle or when there is a natural disaster, especially drought. Then the priests help me control angry subjects. So I have to let them run the temples when things are going well too. I truly believe that there can never be enough temples. There are so many gods and goddesses, and each one likes their own space. How do I know? I have a direct line to the heavens, of course.

We'll leave you the bones, oh great one.

I COMMAND WHERE AND WHEN TEMPLES ARE BUILT. I take an interest in their design too. Grand is good. My best temples are enormous and made of imported stone. Inside, there is a maze of courtyards and rooms. They all lead to a brightly painted inner sanctuary where a statue of the god or goddess rests. Only I and those sly high priests may enter it. They perform rituals and display offerings of food, which some of my loyal subjects say they take home and eat. Unfortunately, with each new temple I build, I lose land to the priests. My son must be careful not to give away too much.

My Greatest Power

My subjects believe that I control the great River Nile, especially when it floods. I make it flood every year during the rainy season, turning desert into fertile land. Just like magic! I am also known as Lord of Two Lands—the Upper Nile and the Lower Nile. I control every drop of water, every grain of soil, and all the crops grown on them.

One of my favorite rules is MAKE THOSE PEASANTS WORK! So after the water has receded, they dig irrigation ditches, plough the soil, and sow and plant. The soil is soft, damp, and fertile. So what's the problem? That great mayor Sennefer, from my southern capital Thebes, knew how to discipline his farm workers:

Do not fail to have things in perfect order. . . . You are not to slack, because I know that you are lazy, and fond of eating in bed.

Mediterranean Sea

The Great Pyramids of Giza

Giza

Bent Pyramid

Western Desert

Red Sea

Eastern Desert

Nile River

Thebes

Valley of the Kings

Of course I'll share—you can have that nice piece of dry, dusty desert.

I INSIST ON BEING A VERY GENEROUS PHARAOH.

I give farms to my lucky nobles. In return, they pay me a lot of crops as taxes. Cereal crops, such as wheat and barley, are my favorites. These feed the people, of course. But I can also export them to other lands. That's why flax is grown too. This is made into a cloth called linen. People from other countries just love to buy our fine linen. That means more riches for me. Now you know why I am so generous.

I WILL TELL YOU WHAT TO EAT!

Peasants and slaves need only simple foods—bread, porridge, vegetables, and fish. But I need a much richer diet. My favorite foods are hippopotamus, crocodile, ostrich, flamingo, and fine fruits such as grapes and pomegranates. Delicious!

I'm sick of crocodile head. Where's the cake?

Fiendish Fact File

- Every June, heavy rains and melting snow from mountains in Ethiopia surged into the River Nile, bringing fertile, silty soil with them.

- Each Egyptian had to shift about 1,000 cubic feet (30 cubic meters) of soil in just ten days to dig irrigation ditches, canals, and dams. That's about the size of a small bedroom.

- The mummified bodies of high priests show that they ate a lot of foods such as cake and goose fat. Many died from their fatty, sugary diets.

Making Cities and Statues

I own all the land in Egypt. This means I can build what I like, where I like. It also means I can stop anyone else from making their own power base—though scheming nobles with their stately homes try! I enjoy climbing to the top floor of my palace in Memphis, one of my greatest cities, and gazing out over the streets below. I think up more ideas for grand palaces, temples, and statues.

I AM THE TOWN PLANNER.

I especially like ordering great structures to be built in and around Memphis. My builders use local white limestone and occasionally yellow sandstone from quarries to the south. My barges haul great lumps of it along a canal that connects the Nile to my mighty Memphis. But make no mistake—all my cities are impressive.

I said yellow sandstone! Knock it down and start again!

I MAKE MASSIVE IMAGES OF MYSELF. I order my masons to carve images showing my great victories in battle. Even if they were not that great, they look as if they were. And I make sure huge, awe-inspiring sculptures of me adorn the land. A towering, triumphant pharaoh means loyalty from the people.

I INSIST THAT POOR SUBJECTS LIVE FAR AWAY FROM MY ROYAL BUILDINGS. Their humble quarters lie in villages on the city's outskirts, thank goodness. Ordinary people only need single-story homes. I allow them to use my clay, water, and straw to make bricks to build them. But these dreadful lowly subjects insist on adding animal dung! Now you know why they live far away from me.

The high priests are always on my case, so **I NEVER FORGET TO HONOR PTAH, THE GOD OF MEMPHIS.** Ptah is a creator god, and his sacred animal is the bull god, Apis. So I make sure that Ptah has a special stall for Apis next to him in the temple. Ptah's high priest is called the chief controller of craftsmen. Huh!

Fiendish Fact File

- Ramesses II was known as The Great Pharaoh. He built temples, statues, and even a new capital city, Pi-Ramesses.

- Pharaohs sometimes plundered stone from old buildings to construct new ones.

- Bulls were buried together in their own cemetery in honor of Ptah.

Building My Tomb

I enjoy watching the progress of my pet project—my own tomb. It is no ordinary tomb, of course, but a massive and spectacular pyramid. This takes a lot of my wealth—and whole armies of builders. But it's worth it. It's the ultimate reminder that I alone will have an afterlife as the sun god Ra. And I alone can grant an afterlife to my loyal subjects.

I WORK CLOSELY WITH ARCHITECTS TO BUILD MY DREAM TOMB. I must end up in a building that stands forever and cannot be robbed. So I pore over the architects' drawings and try to understand all the mathematical calculations. I have many questions. Are there enough secret passages? Is the inner room where I am buried well-hidden? Will my pyramid's sides face the sun and stars properly?

I SIMPLY CANNOT PUT UP WITH LAZINESS OR LATECOMERS.

I mean, laborers only work a ten-day week. Then I give them two days off! My supervisors are very strict and check everyone's work records regularly. Everything is properly logged and written down. Lazy laborers are beaten, hit with a scorpion, or threatened with snakes. It could be a lot worse. After all, I pay them grain and other food rations. They need little else. If the flood fails and food is scarce, the workers dare to complain. Sometimes they even go on strike! I must stop giving them so much to drink.

Oh, no! Not another laborer. I've run out of sting.

Fiendish Fact File

- For each pyramid that was built, about 25,000 workers were hired to dig up the stone, transport it, check its quality, then lay and polish it.

- Laws on animal welfare meant that donkeys used to carry building materials were better-fed than their handlers.

- Ramesses II completed the great Temple of Karnak. He stamped his own logo on lots of temples that he did not build too!

I'M IN CHARGE OF THE BUILDING MATERIALS.

I don't mind using lower-grade limestone for the basic building. A layer of shiny white finer limestone covers it up beautifully. I just wish the quarrymen would dig up more of it. Their copper picks and chisels are sharp and their granite hammers hefty. So what's the problem? They even have passageways between the stone blocks for easy access. I spoil them. I enjoy watching teams of men heaving the stone on sledges, then along ramps that wind around my pyramid. No pain, no gain.

How I Keep Everyone in Place

I have absolute power over all my subjects. But of course, I need people beneath me to help run the country. There's the vizier, with government officials, nobles, and priests at the top level. Much too powerful. Then soldiers, scribes, merchants, craftsmen, and doctors. I like to keep farmers, then servants and slaves, right at the bottom.

The vizier is my very special adviser though he must always remember that I MAKE ALL THE LAWS. My vizier runs the law courts and the government administration though sometimes I override him. I expect him to keep an eye on the nobles and the governors of provinces at the edges of my kingdom. This does not always work. So then I have to send soldiers to sort things out. I sometimes get the feeling that my vizier secretly wants my job.

Keep in your place or I'll poke you with my mace.

MY EVERY WISH IS GRANTED. For example, this week is important as we are preparing for the flood. So I asked my vizier to organize people to cut down the fig trees along the edge of the Nile. Then he had to order the district administrators to dig all the canals. And I mean ALL. In his spare time, he dispatched mayors and village heads to arrange the ploughing and sowing. Any failure will mean I have to send in the troops. And the vizier will be looking for another job.

Now juggle them.

I GIVE MY TOP TEAM RICH REWARDS. Of course, the nobles and priests are rich anyway. They collect gifts for the gods, which often end up in their own pockets. My top administrators are rewarded very well, too, especially when they're dead. I allow them to build a really nice mastaba. This flat-roofed tomb has its own chapel and a steep passage into a burial chamber, which they don't even have to share. A false door allows their spirit to enter a beautifully painted and decorated chamber. Of course, I'm hoping they'll come and work for me in the afterlife.

Fiendish Fact File

- Imhotep was a great vizier who served Pharaoh Djoser (who probably reigned 2630-2611 BCE). Imhotep also designed Djoser's famous Step Pyramid at Saqqara and was made into a god when he died.

- Viziers watched everyone and everything. They were in charge of huge archives containing records of court trials, census lists, and wills.

I am already a god.

The Importance of FACTS

I cannot rule without knowing the facts. So I have an army of scribes to write down lists of trade goods, taxes, accounts, and work records. Having everything in writing means that I know what taxes my subjects owe me and whether they have been paid. This makes me even more rich and powerful. Then there are the mathematicians and astronomers. Without them, I cannot predict when the Nile will flood, and that would be a disaster.

I INSIST THAT MY SCRIBES ARE WELL-TRAINED.

They need to begin lessons at the age of five. Remembering and learning how to write all those hieroglyph symbols of people, animals, and shapes takes a very long time. The children must attend schools regularly. Most are sons, and sometimes daughters, of priests, government officials, and generals. So I expect them to behave themselves. As if! I was a student once . . .

Hmmm. Looks like the pharaoh's nearly dead. Ah well.

I need the hieroglyphs, numbers, maps, and diagrams to be clearly written. **MY SCRIBES MUST USE THE FINEST MATERIALS.** In the palace, everything is written on the best paper, which is made from the pith of the papyrus marsh plant. Fine reed brushes are dipped into black or red ink. My best black ink is made by burning wood or oil, then mixing it with water and gum from the acacia tree. Red ink comes from iron rust. I am very interested in these things. Mostly because I really enjoy seeing my own name on hundreds of scrolls and wall carvings. A pharaoh's name is always written inside a neat rounded shape. So it stands out really well, as it should.

Oy! Check your sandals for donkey dung!

I WILL EMPLOY EVEN THE LOWER CLASSES, basically because we are always desperate for scribes. Most of my scribes are from wealthy families. But some peasant farmers save money to send their children to schools run by priests. I am surprised they can afford it. I need to tax them more. But at least I get a few more scribes. Really intelligent poor people can even end up working in my palace. I reward hard work.

Fiendish Fact File

- By the age of twelve, pupils had to learn more than seven hundred hieroglyphs.

- Scribes worked very long hours, sitting cross-legged on the floor with their palette and inkwells in front of them.

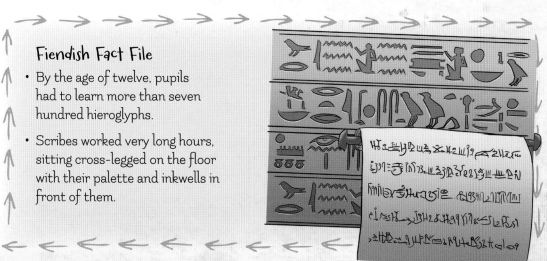

Becoming Very Rich

I am very rich because I own vast lands, collect heavy taxes, and trade our goods with other kingdoms. Sometimes I use my diplomats to get what I want from them. I even call other rulers my brothers. But mostly, I threaten them and take tribute, which means anything I need or like. I operate strict rules on how all this wealth is shared.

MY SHIPS MUST DELIVER THE GOODS.

I have my own fleet of ships and river barges to transport riches from afar. I trade, or raid, cedarwood from Lebanon and gold, ostrich feathers, frankincense, and ivory from Africa's heartland. Obsidian, a gorgeous black stone, is imported from the eastern Mediterranean and the Red Sea. And the blue lapis lazuli stone is hauled all the way from Afghanistan. There are so many other treasures, I am just dripping with them.

Wealth is power, so I HAVE TO BE THE RICHEST PERSON IN EGYPT. However, I allow the nobles, priests, and top administrators a lavish lifestyle, too. It stops them from wanting my job—I hope. I have some respect for scribes, architects, doctors, and artisans. Their skills and learning are necessary to my status and well-being. So I don't mind them being quite wealthy. But the armed forces should feel honored to serve me, so I don't pay them much. As for entertainers, farmers, and laborers, well! They are almost at the bottom of the pay scale with the serfs and slaves.

I MUST ALWAYS LOOK MY BEST. The people expect it. So I spend a lot of wealth and time on my face and hair—a very expensive wig. I cover this with a stunning blue and gold *nemes* cloth that drapes down my neck like a lion's mane. Very powerful! The gold cobra attached to the front of my *nemes* represents Wadjet, the goddess who always protects me. No one else can wear it. My beautiful braided beard (which I wear for ceremonial duties) is made from the best hair. Not my own— the beard is fake!

Designer beard. Perfect.

Fiendish Fact File

• Ancient Egypt traded goods for over 3,000 years. It always tried to control trade, from Europe to the Near East.

• Female pharaohs also wore fake beards and other luxurious clothing and makeup.

Being a Bad Neighbor

It is very important to create balance in my kingdom. To do this, the goddess of justice, Ma'at, works through me. She helps me to stop too much harmony—very dull. This sometimes means that I'm expected to make war on my neighbors, which I am most happy to do. Victory in battle proves that the gods are on my side and makes me popular.

MY NOBLES MUST LEAD A VERY PROFESSIONAL ARMY. *I need a huge, well-trained force to gain more territory. Then I can get more treasures, materials, and, if I'm lucky, hundreds of thousands of cattle. I can also seize thousands of prisoners of war to work as slaves on my building projects. Sometimes other countries are so frightened of me that they just agree to pay me tribute. The trouble is, as my lands get richer, other rulers want to attack them to get rich themselves!*

So you can see why I always need a great army.

Cattle, captives, cattle, captives. What? No gold?

YOU MUST KEEP YOUR WEAPONS SHARP! Our state-of-the-art bronze-tipped spears are so much stronger than the old copper design. Then there are sickle swords, battle-axes, daggers, and piercing bows and arrows. My troops are protected with shields of tough oxhide stretched over a wooden frame. Of course, my foot soldiers follow behind my champion charioteers, who launch surprise attacks on the enemy.

My troops must cross very difficult territory, so I INSIST ON FITNESS. Sometimes I attack Libya to the west, so my navy transports troops by ship. At other times they have to march south to Nubia or north to the Levant. The problem here is the desert. It really gets in the way and slows my troops down to just 14 miles (22 kilometers) a day—if they're lucky. Useless!

Fiendish Fact File

- An Ancient Egyptian army division could be made up of at least four thousand foot soldiers and one thousand charioteers.

- Egyptian troops were terrified of dying on foreign soil and being buried without the right rituals.

- Soldiers had to work even when they were not fighting. They stopped any local unrest and supervised peasants and slaves on building projects.

My Powerful Death

When I die in this life, I will take a lot of wealth to the next one. That includes statues of my most faithful servants and pets. I am just as powerful when I am no longer alive as I turn into Osiris, god of the afterlife. Knowing I will still rule over them when they are dead helps to keep my subjects obedient.

MY FUTURE AS A GOD DEPENDS ON MY BODY BEING PRESERVED.

Death totally ruins the skin. So my body will first be washed in palm wine and spices. My useless brain will be pulled out through my nostrils. My soul rests within my heart, so it will be cut out and weighed to see if I have been a good or a bad pharaoh. Hmmm. Then it will be put back into my body. My other organs will be stored in canopic jars beside me. Natron salts will dry out my body, which will be stuffed with sawdust. I won't feel a thing. My skin will be treated with wax, gum, and cedar tree oil, then wrapped in linen bandages. A priest will touch my eyes, ears, nose, mouth, hands, and feet so they will work in the afterlife.

I INSIST YOU MOURN FOR ME! I will be carried to my royal barge and transported to my pyramid. Many other boats will follow, filled with dignitaries and mourners. There must be processions with bands playing and a lot of harp music. Women must scream, cry, tear their hair out, and make lament for Osiris, which, of course, will be me.

My hair's ruined!

THE POOR MUST NEVER BE GRANTED GRAND FUNERALS.

They can't afford them anyway. White linen cloth is good enough for them. Their procession takes a very long time. That's because their bodies are carried way beyond the city, toward the setting sun. Luckily for me, they are buried quickly beneath the desert sand. That means their mourners can soon get back to work.

Fiendish Fact File

- It took forty days for a body filled with natron to dry out before it was mummified.

- Balls of linen were stuffed into the empty eye sockets.

- Vultures and jackals dug beneath the sand and rocks placed on top of graves to eat the bodies of the poor.

YUM! Tastier than a pharaoh.

Gods and Goddesses

I shall of course turn into the god Osiris when I die. Below you can meet some other gods. They are all depicted in different ways.

PTAH created the world just by thinking and talking. Imagine that! He holds a rod because he is the patron god of craftsmen, which means he protects them. He does not need any protection himself because he has a fearsome wife.

SEKHMET is Ptah's powerful lion-headed wife. She destroyed the enemies of their son, Nefertum. She turned on the enemies of Ra, the sun god too. I always give her expensive offerings such as hippo meat.

RA is the god of the sun. He has a falcon's head surrounded by a great disc, which represents the sun. He is known as Atum in the evening and Khepri in the morning. Very complicated. Khepri is depicted as a scarab or dung beetle.

HORUS is the god of the sky and looks like a falcon. I really like Horus because he is the protector of pharaohs. Many people believe that a pharaoh is Horus. I like that idea.

THOTH is the very brainy god of knowledge and writing. He weighs the hearts of the dead to judge them. Then he writes down the judgement for Osiris. Egypt has millions of mummified baboons and ibis birds to honor him.

OSIRIS is the god of the afterlife. A pharaoh turns into Osiris when he dies. Osiris was drowned by another god, Seth, who tore his body into pieces. Surprisingly, Osiris is also the god of new life springing from the Nile flood every year.

SETH is known as the Red god— the god of the desert sands. He brings great thunderstorms and violence. No one knows what kind of creature he is. His body looks like a graceful greyhound, but his head with its square ears could be anything.

TEFNUT is the goddess of rain and cloud. She has the head of a lioness, which makes her look rather angry. She became a goddess when Ra, the sun god, spat her out. I think that would make me angry too.

SOBEK has the face of a crocodile. He guards our water channels and the great River Nile. There are pools inside his temple where snapping crocodiles swim. Sobek likes to eat a lot of meat.

ANUBIS looks like a jackal, or wild dog. Jackals prowl around graveyards. So jackal-headed Anubis protects us when we are dead. He is also the god of preserving dead bodies. I certainly would never argue with him.

29

Ten More Fiendish Pharaohs

These early Egyptian kings and pharaohs are also a little bit fiendish. We know about them from writings in tombs and temples.

1 Menes (about 2925 BCE), probably also known as Narmer, may have united Upper and Lower Egypt. The historian Manetho wrote that Menes ruled for sixty-two years and was killed by a hippopotamus. Others said that dogs and crocodiles chewed him up.

2 Khufu (reigned about 2589–2566 BCE) was a real tyrant. It is said that he raised taxes when his people were starving. He built the Great Pyramid of Giza, putting Egypt in debt. It took 2,300,000 bricks and twenty-three years to complete.

3 Pepi II or Neferkare (possibly reigned 2247–2216 BCE) hated flies, so his workers were coated in honey to attract them. But mosquitoes, bees, and wasps also made a beeline for the sweet bodies, adding to the workers' discomfort.

4 Hatshepsut (reigned 1473–1458 BCE) shared duties with her stepson and nephew, Thutmose III. But she kept him in his place. She chose officials who followed her rules to make Egypt rich through trade. She also wore the false beard and clothing of male pharaohs.

5 Thutmose III (reigned 1479–1425 BCE) won every battle in seventeen military campaigns. He expanded Egypt from Syria to Sudan. Thutmose captured many prisoners and sacrificed them at the Temple of Amun. He also built more than fifty temples.

6 Ramesses I only ruled for a little over one year (1292–1290 BCE) before he died. His body was thrown quickly into a grave. Then it was dug up again. His remains were found in Atlanta, Georgia. But in 2003 they were returned to Egypt.

7 Seti I (reigned 1290–1279 BCE) was a mighty conqueror and made Egypt rich. He strengthened defenses around the kingdom, dug wells, opened up mines, and repaired decaying temples.

8 Ramesses II (reigned 1279–1213 BCE) went on military campaigns with his father Seti from the age of fourteen. He was a great builder—his two most famous temples are carved out of a cliff in Nubia. He ruled for so long that people thought the world might end when he died.

9 Ramesses III (reigned 1187–1156 BCE) wiped out or enslaved Libyan troops during an invasion of Egypt. But one of his wives, Queen Tiy, planned his death. In 2012, scans on his mummified body showed a knife wound in his neck.

10 Cleopatra (reigned 51–30 BCE) was the last and perhaps most famous pharaoh. At different times she held power with her two brothers and son. They were all called Ptolemy. She presented herself as the goddess Isis, who was associated with kingship. From 32 BCE, she was at war with Rome and was defeated at the Battle of Actium. Egypt became part of the Roman Empire and the pharaohs were no more.

INDEX

afterlife, 6, 16, 19, 26, 29
Anubis, 29
army, 24–25

beards and makeup, 6, 23, 30
becoming a pharaoh, 8–9
buildings, 14–15

Cleopatra, 31
clothes, 9, 23

death, 26–27

floods, 12–13, 17, 19–20, 29

goddesses, 6, 10–11, 23–24, 28–29, 31
gods, 6, 10–11, 15–16, 19, 24, 26, 28–29

Hatshepsut, 30
Horus, 28

Khufu, 30

laws, 17–18

Memphis, 14–15
mummification, 13, 26–27, 29, 31

Nile River, 12–14, 19–20, 29–30

Osiris, 26–29

peasants and poor people, 9, 12–13, 15, 17, 21, 25, 27
Ptah, 15, 28
pyramids, 16–17, 19, 27, 30

Ra, 10, 16, 28
Ramesses II, 9, 15, 17, 31

scribes, 6–7, 18, 20–22
statues, 11, 14–15, 26

temples, 10–11, 14–15, 17, 29–30
tombs, 16–27, 19, 30
trade, 20, 22–23, 30
tribute, 22, 24

viziers, 6–7, 18–19

wealth, 8, 16, 21–23, 26
weapons, 25

The Author

Catherine Chambers was born in Adelaide, South Australia, and brought up in England. She earned a degree in African History and Swahili at the School of Oriental and African Studies, London. Catherine has written about 130 titles for children and young adults, mainly non-fiction, and she enjoys seeking out intriguing facts for her non-fiction titles.

The Illustrator

Ryan Pentney lives and works in Norwich, UK. Growing up in the 1990s, he was surrounded by iconic cartoons, comics, and books that have remained a passion with him. Inspired by these childhood heroes as well as more modern works, Ryan creates his own characters and stories in the hope of inspiring the next generation. He uses the latest technology and traditional techniques to make stylized digital artworks.